TECH
bytes

HIGH-TECH

The Internet of Things

by Carrie Clickard

NORWOODHOUSE PRESS

Cover: The Internet of Things puts users in control of a wide variety of devices connected by computer networks.

Norwood House Press
P.O. Box 316598
Chicago, Illinois 60631

For information regarding Norwood House Press, please visit our website at: www.norwoodhousepress.com or call 866-565-2900.

Content Consultant: Josh Siegel, Research Scientist, Massachusetts Institute of Technology

Hardcover ISBN: 978-1-59953-939-3
Paperback ISBN: 978-1-68404-218-0

Library of Congress Cataloging-in-Publication Data

Names: Clickard, Carrie (Carrie L.), author.
Title: The internet of things / by Carrie Clickard.
Description: Chicago, Illinois : Norwood House Press, [2018] | Series: Tech bytes. High-tech | Includes bibliographical references and index.
Identifiers: LCCN 2018004393 (print) | LCCN 2018011781 (ebook) | ISBN 9781684042234 (ebook) | ISBN 9781599539393 (hardcover : alk. paper) | ISBN 9781684042180 (pbk. : alk. paper)
Subjects: LCSH: Internet of things--Juvenile literature.
Classification: LCC TK5105.8857 (ebook) | LCC TK5105.8857 .C56 2018 (print) | DDC 004.67/8--dc23
LC record available at https://lccn.loc.gov/2018004393

312N—072018
Manufactured in the United States of America in North Mankato, Minnesota.

CONTENTS

Note: Words that are **bolded** in the text are defined in the glossary.

CHAPTER 1

Tech Support for Life

It is 6:00 a.m. on the day of Jenny's big soccer game. She is still in bed dreaming of a big win. But all around her, the Internet of Things hums with activity. Her smart alarm clock checked her online schedule last night. It is set to give her an extra half hour of sleep. Her older brother, Jasper, used all the milk for a smoothie before his morning run. So, the refrigerator sends a text alert to Dad. Dad picks up a gallon on his way home from the donut shop.

Yawning over her morning coffee, Mom sees her phone buzz. There is highway construction on the way to Jenny's game. Jenny needs to get up earlier. With a tap on the screen, Mom adjusts Jenny's alarm. Meanwhile, Dad is brushing his teeth. His smart toothbrush records every stroke. He watches the weather report displayed in the smart glass mirror. A message pops up on the mirror from the laundry room. Jenny's uniform is now crisp, clean, and dry.

Buzzes from both their phones send Mom and Dad scurrying in two directions. Mom heads to the smart oven. It is preheated and ready for the breakfast casserole. Dad's phone says the car's tires are fine and the oil level is good. But he has forgotten to fill up with gas. On his way to the car, he bumps into Jasper. An alert on Jasper's fitness bracelet reminded him of Jenny's game.

Soon, Jenny's alarm finally goes off. She stumbles into the kitchen for breakfast. Then she puts on her clean uniform and climbs into the car. Everyone's relieved as Jenny rushes onto the field in plenty of time for a great game day. All of this was possible because of the Internet of Things.

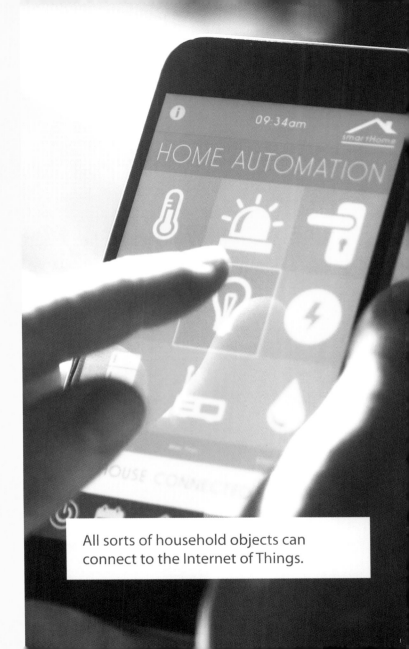

All sorts of household objects can connect to the Internet of Things.

What Is the Internet of Things?

The Internet of Things (IoT) is made up of all the physical devices connected to the Internet. These devices send, receive, or exchange data over computer networks. Long before smartphones and other smart devices, people connected machines to computers. Each connection was a small step toward today's IoT.

In 1971, banks connected their computers to the first ATMs. Customers could access their money without going inside the bank. In 1982, four students at Carnegie Mellon University connected a soda vending machine to the school's network. They installed **microswitches** that sensed how many bottles were in each stack. Then they wrote a program that displayed how many bottles were left in the machine. The program also showed how long the bottles had been in the machine. Students could run the program from any computer connected to the school's network. The students had created the first Internet-connected appliance. You can still find their soda vending machine on the web today.

In 1973, inventor Charles Walton patented a small computer chip with an antenna. It sent data wirelessly between objects connected to a computer network. The invention was called a radio frequency identification device (RFID). Today, billions of devices contain RFID chips. Chips can be active or passive. Active chips require a battery. Passive ones do not. They allow the devices to communicate without being physically connected.

The IoT took a big step forward in 1989. Dan Lynch was the president of the Interop Internet networking trade show. Lynch challenged rising star programmer John Romkey to connect a toaster to the Internet. If he could, Romkey would get star billing at next year's show.

RFID chips can be found in lots of everyday items, including security tags for clothing.

Want Some Coffee with That Toast?

At the University of Cambridge, scientists hated walking from their labs to the coffee pot just to find it empty. In 1993, they set up a camera in the coffee room. It took pictures three times a minute. The scientists wrote software that put those pictures on their internal computer network. Then everyone could know when the pot was full.

Romkey set to work with the help of Simon Hackett. They connected a toaster to a power switch. Then they connected the switch to the printer port of a laptop. With a click on the keyboard, the programmers could turn on the toaster. They could also control the toaster remotely. They took the toaster to the 1990 Interop Internet networking show. It was an instant hit.

IoT in the 1990s and 2000s

The Internet toaster was just the beginning. IBM created the first smartphone, called Simon, in 1994. It had a touch screen and could send e-mail and faxes. Radio stations began broadcasting over the Internet.

By 1999, the number of objects and services connected to the Internet had

Apple founder Steve Jobs presents the first iPhone in January 2007.

grown very large. In that year, innovator and technology expert Kevin Ashton called it "the Internet of Things."

Since then, the IoT has grown at an amazing rate. By 2000, wireless **hot spots** had popped up in coffee shops, restaurants, and malls. Smart objects could now connect to the IoT in public. In 2000, a Japanese company invented the first smart refrigerator. Two years later, researcher Kevin Warwick agreed to have an RFID chip implanted in his arm. The chip let him open doors and turn on lights and computers without touching them.

Then, in 2007, the iPhone hit the market. It was the first popular monitor temperature, energy use, and traffic. It also has an underground waste system that automatically sucks garbage down and out of homes.

In a few short decades, the IoT has grown to include cars, toothbrushes, and clothes. It also includes shoes, trash cans, and doorbells. Billions of other objects make up the IoT, too.

No Typing Required

Before smart objects were connected directly to the Internet, humans had to enter information online. People typed it or took a digital picture. They pressed record buttons and scanned bar codes.

Now, digital sensors observe, record, upload, and analyze. Humans do not have to lift a finger. The sensors can

smartphone. Since that year, more than 1.2 billion iPhones have been sold. The demand for more IoT objects rose.

Soon, whole cities were building IoT networks. In 2009, the Songdo International Business District opened in South Korea. It is a smart city with businesses and homes. It has **sensors** to

The IoT and Big Data

Smart devices on the IoT run nearly constantly. They collect a lot of data about their users and the world around them. This includes users' names and locations. It can include photos and videos. Sometimes, it includes private information, such as credit card or bank account information. This massive amount of information is called *big data*. Organizations use big data for lots of reasons. Companies use it to learn more about their customers. They can improve their products or offer special deals. Hospitals use big data to improve patient care. Cities use it to make public transportation more efficient.

measure many different things. They can observe and record location, weather, movement, temperature, environment, and size. All that data is uploaded to the **cloud** over an IoT platform. A platform is a shared computer language similar to a computer's operating system. The platform allows devices to communicate. They share, analyze, and act on the data they have collected.

By acting on their own, smart objects make the IoT more independent. They can provide more information and more answers with less work by people. Smart objects can share information faster and more reliably than people can. IoT data is not entered on a keyboard. So, there are no typing errors. IoT devices cannot lie or forget. The data they collect is as close

A smart mirror analyzes a woman's skin at a technology show in Japan in 2016.

しみ (2016/10/03)

セレクト

2016/10/03

化粧品

終了

to the truth as possible. Users can attach sensors to nearly any object that exists.

How the IoT Helps Humans

Nearly all the objects now connected to the IoT have existed for a long time. They just have not had sensors or shared data until recently. Why does the world need umbrellas, alarm clocks, or trash cans to connect to the Internet?

Everyone loves convenience, comfort, and reliability. Families want more time to relax and have fun. Smart objects can do some of their boring, time-consuming work. Smart refrigerators and cupboards can automatically reorder food or medications. Smart mirrors display the weather and daily schedules and remind children to brush their teeth. Alarm clocks talk to online calendars and pick the right time to go off.

Computers can repeat the same task without making the slightest change. Humans will never be able to achieve the same level of accuracy alone. But the IoT can help. Learning to play guitar takes a lot of practice. A new fabric sleeve slips over the neck of a guitar. It has **circuit boards** on the back and lights on the front. It is connected to the Internet. Users select a song online. The sleeve lights up where players need to put their fingers to play the song.

A smart baseball bat can track a player's swing. It sends data through the Internet to a computer. Software analyzes the swing and helps players improve their game. Shoes made for runners connect

wirelessly to the web. The shoes send directions to the runners' phones. They can also track distance and runners' heartbeats. Self-driving cars can respond faster and avoid accidents.

The IoT helps the environment, too. Smart lightbulbs turn on only when people enter a room. This saves energy and money. Smart trash cans call for

A fleet of Google's self-driving cars on display in Mountain View, California

pickup when they are full. This helps save gasoline and use less oil. Even plants and soil have been connected to the IoT. Sensors in the dirt provide farmers with data that helps them use less water. Farmers place other sensors in their water wells. The sensors send data to the farmers' computers. The data tells farmers if water levels are getting low.

Smart devices and their sensors make all these improvements possible. No wonder the IoT is expanding in hundreds of new directions. Businesses and universities are rushing to keep up with all the possibilities. Some researchers call the IoT the beginning of the next **Industrial Revolution**.

CHAPTER 2

Growing Pains

The IoT is growing a little too fast. According to technology company Intel, the IoT will soon include more than 200 billion smart objects. Businesses and researchers are scrambling to keep up. They need to solve challenges before the IoT is everywhere.

It's Getting Crowded in Here!

Every online computer and object must have its own IP (Internet Protocol) address.

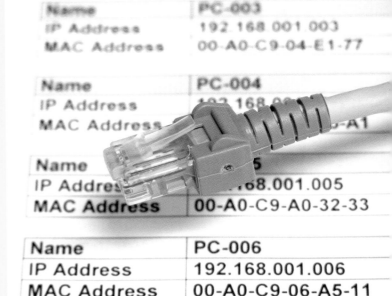

Name	PC-003
IP Address	192.168.001.003
MAC Address	00-A0-C9-04-E1-77

Name	PC-004
IP Address	192.168.0
MAC Address	-A1

Name	5
IP Address	.68.001.005
MAC Address	00-A0-C9-A0-32-33

Name	PC-006
IP Address	192.168.001.006
MAC Address	00-A0-C9-06-A5-11

IP addresses identify computers and objects online.

Every object in the IoT, including robotic lawnmowers, has an IP address.

This address identifies and locates the smart object on the Internet. It is similar to a home's street address. An IP address is a string of numbers separated into four sections by periods. An example IP address is 192.168.0.1. Each one of those four sections has a number between 0 and 255. This system created 4 billion IP addresses.

Hey, Turn Down the IoT!

In 2015, an argument broke out between smart lawnmowers and smart telescopes. A smart lawnmower company used wireless beacons to connect the lawnmowers to the Internet. The beacons were stakes driven into the ground. But the beacons used the same radio frequency as important research telescopes. The lawnmowers' signals interfered with the telescopes. Astronomers had trouble tracking star formation. The astronomers wanted the lawnmowers off their frequency completely. The lawnmower company wanted free use of any frequency. In the end, the companies compromised. The lawnmower company could install the beacons. But they could only be 24 inches (61 cm) off the ground.

But the IoT outgrew these addresses. By 2011, all the IP addresses were taken. So, in 2012, a new IP system launched. It had been in development since 1998. Called IPv6, it uses much longer numbers. This allows for more unique number combinations to be created. With IPv6, there are 340 undecillion available addresses. That's 340 followed by 36 zeros! The IoT should not run out of IP addresses anytime soon.

DID YOU KNOW? ?

There are 100 IPv6 addresses for every atom on Earth.

Too Many Systems

Computers use different hardware and operating systems. It is the same for smart objects. Thousands of computer applications run smart objects. All of these operating systems must talk to one another. One of the IoT's big challenges is making all these different systems communicate properly.

 DID YOU KNOW?

In 1950, Ray Bradbury wrote "The Veldt." It is a short story about what could go wrong with a smart house.

Visible Data

As the IoT grows, so do privacy concerns. Every minute, users transfer 639,800 gigabytes of data online. Some of that data is personal. It includes names, addresses, and even photos. Imagine a smart house that knows when a family leaves for work to control the thermostat. Who sees that information? Where does this data get stored? When a device reorders medicine, who knows about that? Can the data be sold to companies? How do we know data is safe?

Companies that sell smart objects can protect users' data. So can the companies that provide storage in the cloud. **Firewalls** and intruder-detection software keep hackers from accessing data. So do passwords and **authentication** systems.

Encryption stops hackers from reading any data they steal. Companies are developing new **routers** and devices that can serve as network security scanners, too.

Seafood, Anyone?

These security features help protect data. But hackers, spam, and viruses are still problems for the IoT. For example, one university's smart vending machines and lampposts suddenly started searching the Internet. The objects were looking for information on seafood. Hackers had instructed thousands of smart objects to make hundreds of searches every 15 minutes. It brought the university's computer system to a standstill. Until the

What Is a Hacker?

Billions of smart objects are vulnerable to being attacked by hackers. Hackers are people who gain access to computer systems illegally. They may decode passwords or find a weakness in the system's firewall. Once they are in, hackers usually install software on the computer system. The software may record a computer user's keyboard strokes. Or, it may lock down the entire system until the user pays the hackers money to regain access. The IoT provides hackers billions of possible ways to access computer systems. Without strong protection, any smart device is vulnerable to hackers.

Hackers disrupted a German railway system in 2017. Screens that normally showed railway information instead said *Bitte Aushangfahrplan beachten*, or "Please note the timetable." Passengers had to look elsewhere for the information.

searches stopped, the university's computer system could not function.

Another hacker pulled off a global stunt. Many smart object owners never change their devices' default passwords. These are the passwords that come preset on devices and are the same for each object. The hacker used these passwords to access the objects. He sent spam e-mails around the world using the connected devices to relay his messages. Law enforcement tried to catch the hacker. But the messages traced back to thousands of refrigerators.

In 2017, a sixth grader proved how easily smart toys could be hacked. All it took was a laptop, an IoT teddy bear, and a small programmable computer. In just a few minutes, the sixth grader made the bear light up and speak.

Even smart toys are vulnerable to hackers when they are part of the IoT.

These examples are a little funny. But they are also serious problems. Sometimes the answer is as simple as changing passwords. More often, owners must update software or replace a device. But it is unclear who is responsible for making sure these software updates happen. Is it the device owner or the

To protect data, companies must secure their computer systems.

manufacturer? Criminals can hack into city infrastructure, causing accidents and chaos. Security and privacy problems will not stop the IoT from growing. But it is one more reason the IoT is not everywhere just yet.

CHAPTER 3

The World of Smart Objects

Billions of smart objects are already connected to the IoT. Most of the smart objects on the IoT today are not in family homes. They are in factories, public buildings, and businesses. The data they upload help lower costs, improve quality, and keep people safer.

In the Factory

Factories use sensors to measure weight. The sensors are attached to the factories'

Sensors in factory warehouses help companies keep track of supplies.

supply containers. When a container is too light, workers get notified over the Internet. Sensors can track temperature so food items do not spoil. Movement and location sensors let managers track both supplies and finished inventory. Movement sensors can be part of factory security. If supplies are moving when the factory is closed, it could indicate a robbery. The sensors help keep costs down for manufacturers. Sensors can also tell machines and operators when to perform a task.

DID YOU KNOW?

By 2024, nearly all transportation companies will use the IoT to track shipments, plan and change driver routes, and provide real-time data on accurate estimated times of arrival.

On the Road

The IoT is already helping improve transportation. Data from IoT-linked trucks tracks driving speeds and habits. This encourages drivers to be safer on the road. Sensors can scan for trucks on the road ahead. They can follow these trucks automatically to save fuel and increase safety. Other sensors that monitor engine parts for stress and damage help avoid breakdowns. Some companies use IoT location and traffic monitoring systems to warn drivers of traffic jams and accidents. This means fewer hours on the road. It saves gas, too.

Around the Town

It might be hard to spot the smart objects in a city. A lot of what they do is invisible. But they can make a big difference. Smart street lights turn on only when cars or people are nearby. This saves electricity. Connected trash cans silently signal when they are full and ready for pickup. In the park, smart sprinklers turn on only when plants need water. Parking lots at airports and malls send maps of open spots to smartphones or a car's GPS. Sensors posted on lampposts can monitor air or noise pollution.

A man uses a smart trashcan in Philadelphia, Pennsylvania.

The IoT at Home

In 2016, 31 million homes in North America were connected to the IoT. In the coming years, researchers believe more than half the houses in North America will be smart homes.

What makes a house smart? Smart homes start with sensors and an

Smart mirrors can give people a quick look at weather, traffic, and the news.

Mirror, Mirror, on the Web?

It is 7:30 a.m. The alarm just went off. But the bus comes at 7:50. No time to check the weather or text messages. There is barely time for hair and tooth brushing. Life can be just a little easier with the IoT and a connected mirror. Sensors read when someone is standing in front of it. The mirror displays the information you choose, including weather, time, and messages. It even senses your smile or frown to greet you appropriately. Smart devices will not solve the problem of needing the alarm clock. But they can help you get ready for your day.

Internet connection. Doors, windows, lights, and thermostats can connect to the IoT. Smartphones can control the whole house. Lights turn off when movement and temperature sensors say the house is empty. Smart window blinds measure sunlight and open or close automatically. Moisture sensors turn off the lawn sprinklers if it starts to rain. If a door or window is opened when no one is home, homeowners know instantly.

IoT Companions

Internet-connected robots already exist. Many perform dangerous, difficult, or dull work. But brand-new robots may offer something even more complex: companionship. Smart objects can

Paro the seal is an IoT companion for older people in Japan.

become a favorite companion of older people in Japan. The smart object can detect sound and light. It detects and responds to its owner's touch and posture.

Smart Health Care

The IoT is being used in health care, too. Wearable devices help people with diabetes track their blood sugar levels. The devices automatically send data to the wearer's doctors. A similar watch is also available for people with heart disease. It monitors heart rate and the

schedule appointments and connect to social media. They can ask owners if they would like to video chat with family and friends. The smart object analyzes data from its interactions with its owner. It learns to make suggestions about what the owner may want to read or watch on TV.

One of these smart objects is Paro the seal. It is a smart plush animal. Paro has

When Your Geranium Asks for a Drink

Plants can benefit from the IoT, too. Sensors that measure moisture and temperature can turn ordinary plants into smart plants. The sensors text owners when plants need to be moved to a sunnier or shadier spot. Plants can also ask for a drink of water. Gardens can remind owners when they need to be weeded. Farmers are already using the IoT to quickly target field pests. The IoT also reduces the amount of water needed to grow their crops. An avocado farmer in California uses the IoT to monitor his plants. It has reduced water use by approximately 75 percent in young trees. That is healthy not just for the plants. It is healthy for the planet, too.

amount of oxygen in the blood. A smart patch attaches directly to a patient's skin. It collects data such as breathing rate and skin temperature. Then, it sends this valuable information to the patient's doctors.

Connecting Smart Objects

To connect an object to the IoT, you need four things. First, a sensor attaches to the object. Many smart objects contain their own sensors. The sensor reads what you want to measure. Second, software reads the sensor's data. Third, a Wi-Fi, cellular,

Smartwatches send data back to an app, which gives feedback to the wearer.

or Bluetooth connection transmits data to the cloud. Then the software makes a decision on what to do next. Last, the software takes action based on the data collected.

Imagine you want to know how much food is left in your turtle's dish. First, attach a sensor to the bottom of the turtle's filled food dish. The sensor will measure the bowl's weight. Software reads the data from the sensor. It uploads the dish's weight to the cloud once an hour. Then another software program analyzes the data. If the food dish's weight drops below a certain level, it could send you a text message.

You may also want to know if the weight of the food bowl stays the same for more than 12 hours. That could mean your turtle is not eating. The software would send you a different text message. More advanced systems could connect to your turtle's food dispenser. Instead of sending a text, it would automatically pour more food in the turtle's bowl. Companies already sell dog and cat dishes that do exactly that.

German scientists use the IoT to study tree health.

CHAPTER 4

Dreaming Big

The IoT is very big already. It connects billions of smart devices to each other. It is hard to imagine what more it could do. Yet inventors and IoT programmers keep announcing uses for this technology. Future opportunities are popping up in some surprising places. It is likely that in the coming years, the IoT will continue to spread into new areas around the world. It will help scientists, companies, and everyday people.

The Internet of Sharks

Shark attacks were a problem in Western Australia. A new IoT company decided it could do something to help. The company developed a shark monitoring system. It used the Internet, **sonar** sensors, and shark identification software.

The sonar sensors attach to the ocean floor. They scan for movement in the water. When something passes a sensor, the sensor records the movement. Then it uploads the data to the Internet. A special

The IoT is helping scientists prevent shark attacks in Australia.

software program identifies the species by the way it swims. When something shows sharklike swimming patterns, software sends lifeguards a text alert.

The Department of Fisheries of Western Australia uses another method of tracking sharks. It attaches acoustic tags to sharks. The tags broadcast sharks' locations, like the GPS in a car. When a shark swims past sonar sensors, the data goes directly to Twitter. More than 300 sharks had been tagged by 2014. Scientists use the data to study the sharks.

Neither system is perfect. The locations and number of sonar sensors are limited. Some sharks get missed. But as IoT technology improves, so will shark research.

New Bedford fishing boats may soon use IoT technologies.

Helping Commercial Fishermen

The IoT is already helping farmers. Soon, it may be helping commercial fishermen, too. New Bedford, Massachusetts, is one of the top US fishing ports. Port director Edward Anthes-Washburn hoped in 2016 that the IoT would help fishermen locate and track catches. He imagined sensors on the 500 fishing boats in his port. These sensors would track the temperature and quality of the water. Certain temperatures and qualities attract certain types of fish. With the data, fishermen would have a better idea of where their next catch swims.

Screenless Devices

Some IoT inventors predict computer screens will eventually go away. Smart objects will communicate with the cloud automatically. No one will touch a button or swipe a screen.

One place inventors imagine this happening is right inside our closets. Researchers at the University of California, Berkeley, are working on a new kind of thread that responds to electricity. When the current changes, so does the color of thread. A tug on a sleeve could change a shirt's color. The user would know that a certain color would represent data coming from the IoT. For instance, the thread turning red could represent that the thermostat is detecting a high temperature in the room.

Some experts even believe that in the future, people will be able to access the IoT directly through their vision. Implanted artificial eyes could put data into a person's field of view. This technology is a long way off. Today's head-mounted displays and glasses with tiny built-in screens are early steps along the path to accessing the IoT with a simple glance.

Smart Socks

Socks already do a lot of work keeping feet dry and warm. Tomorrow's socks are going to do much more. One IoT company has created smart running socks. The smart socks have very thin sensors woven right into their fabric. The sensors measure how far and how long someone runs. They also measure a runner's speed.

After they collect all this data, the socks upload the data to online coaching software. Runners can view the data on

Sci-Fi Wearables Become Reality

On the hit science fiction franchise Star Trek, space explorers wear devices called universal translators. The devices translate alien languages in real time. The explorers can communicate easily with alien species. Today, companies are working on universal translators for human languages. Waverly Labs is developing a translation earpiece called Pilot. When one person speaks, the earbud listens. It sends what it hears to an app, which translates the language. The app sends the translation to the earpiece. Finally, the earpiece says the translation to the wearer. The translation takes just a second. People who speak different languages can have a seamless conversation.

The technology company Google demonstrated a similar device in 2017. Its new earbuds, working with a smartphone in the user's pocket and an Internet connection, were able to translate a conversation between a Swedish speaker and an English speaker. These computer translation technologies are not perfect yet, but they are improving all the time.

their smartphones, and they can receive tips on how to improve via e-mail. The software gives advice on how to avoid injuries, based on a person's running style. It even tracks how far a person has run in a pair of running shoes and recommends when it is time to buy a new pair.

Saving Endangered Species

Seventy percent of the world's rhinos live in South Africa. However, their numbers are shrinking. With a zebra's help, the IoT may make a difference.

Zebras and rhinos are often at the same watering holes or grazing areas.

A zebra in South Africa wears a motion-sensor collar.

? DID YOU KNOW?

"LoRaWAN" stands for Long Range Wide Area Network. Scientists use LoRaWAN IoT devices to track wildlife populations. The devices have a range of up to 30 miles (48 km).

Researchers noticed zebras scared by people act differently than zebras scared by animals. They teamed up with IBM to put IoT motion sensor collars on zebras. The sensors upload each zebra's movements to the web. The data is compared to known patterns. If the pattern

Honeybees and the IoT

Honeybees pollinate 75 percent of the food humans eat. When scientists estimated one-third of the honeybee population had died, they were concerned. Now, beekeepers use the IoT to prevent colony collapse. This is when honeybees die off rapidly. Beekeepers use weight sensors under hives and a wireless connection. If the hive changes weight by a large amount, sensors alert the beekeeper. The keeper checks the hives to see what is wrong. Keepers also added sensors to track noise and light levels. Hopefully, the data will help scientists learn how to protect the bees.

matches "scared by animals," nothing happens. But if the pattern matches "scared by people," software sends out a warning. Game wardens can scare off the poachers and save the rhinos.

A Member of the Family

Many people already video chat on their smartphones. Seeing a smiling face can be a nice pick-me-up. But it does not feel like callers are in the same room. The designers of the Ohmni robot hope to change that. It takes companionship smart objects to a new, innovative level. The smart device does not look like a human. But its designers hope it can feel like a friend or family member is right in the room.

Some beekeepers use the IoT to track the health of their beehives.

The Ohmni contains a camera, a microphone, and a tablet that is connected to the Internet. The tablet is on top of a pole. The pole is attached to a base with wheels. The owner can control the robot. But so can friends and family members with a special app. They use the app to control the Ohmni, even when they are far away. They can call in to video chat. They can move the smart object around the room. This can make it feel as if the caller is right there in the room. The designers hope the Ohmni will be used to keep up with friends and family. The robot may have uses in the medical field, too.

The IoT may make many jobs unneeded, including taxi driving.

? DID YOU KNOW?

By 2030, some experts predict most Americans will own a self-driving car.

Future Thoughts

According to IoT experts, in the future, everything that can be smart will be smart. Eric Schmidt of Google agrees. Eventually, he believes people will not directly experience the Internet as they do today. He says, "There will be so many IP addresses, so many devices, sensors, things that you are wearing . . . that you won't even sense it."

Will a larger IoT mean fewer jobs for people? Like any new technology, the IoT changes the way we live and work. Some data-collecting jobs will go away. But new jobs will appear: programming the IoT, designing sensors, and creating new smart objects. Data from the IoT will help researchers in fields such as medicine and astronomy. There may not be fewer jobs with a larger IoT. But there will be different jobs.

What happens when devices lose their Internet connections? If you disconnect a smart object, it still does

Smart refrigerators often feature large touchscreens that put a wealth of information at a user's fingertips.

In the future, your experience with the IoT will be seamless.

its normal work. A refrigerator will still keep food fresh. But it won't notify you if you are out of milk. A baseball bat will still swing. But it will not give you tips to improve your form. Factories may run more slowly. People may need to do some work by hand.

Smart houses will make our daily lives easier. Smart cars will drive us quickly and safely wherever we want to go. Smart lights, trash cans, and watering systems will reduce waste. No one is sure how quickly these devices will spread across the globe. However, as the IoT evolves, it is sure to become an important part of life for billions of people around the world.

? DID YOU KNOW?

By 2027, the electrical grid will be part of the IoT, increasing efficiency.

GLOSSARY

authentication (aw-then-tuh-KAY-shun): The process of allowing a computer or device to connect to a network and verify its identity.

circuit boards (SUR-kut BORDZ): Cards with electrical circuits used to expand a computer's capabilities.

cloud (KLOWD): Data processing and storage space on the Internet.

encryption (in-KRIP-shun): The scrambling of computer code and messages to make them harder to read for hackers.

firewalls (FY-ur-walz): Hardware and software systems that protect computer networks from hackers.

hot spots (HAWT spots): Places where wireless Internet is available.

Industrial Revolution (in-DUS-tree-ul rev-oh-LOO-shun): A period in which popular technologies rapidly change and develop.

microswitches (MY-krow-swi-chuz): Small switches that can be rapidly turned on and off.

routers (ROUW-turz): Devices that help data move across the Internet.

sensors (SEN-surz): Devices that detect heat, light, sound, pressure, or other changes in their environments.

sonar (SO-nahr): A method for detecting sound waves underwater to determine the location, size, and motion of objects.

FOR MORE INFORMATION

Books

Carla Mooney. *Wearable Robots*. Chicago, IL: Norwood House, 2017. Wearable robots help people move a limb, lift heavy objects, and even walk. Get the details on these cutting-edge technologies.

Heather Lyons. *Programming Games and Animation*. Minneapolis, MN: Lerner Publications, 2017. Learn the basics of how to program a computer game. This book gives step-by-step instructions for young programmers.

John Keefe. *Make: Family Projects for Smart Objects: Tabletop Projects That Respond to Your World*. San Francisco, CA: Maker Media, 2016. Make your own smart objects with this guide for beginners, written in easy-to-understand language.

Websites

Beanz: The Magazine for Kids, Code, and Computer Science (https://www.kidscodecs.com/) This website has hundreds of articles and resources on computers, coding, and the IoT.

How the Internet Works (https://www.youtube.com/watch?v=Dxcc6ycZ73M) Ever wonder who created the Internet or who's in charge? Learn all this and more in this YouTube video series from Code.org.

INDEX

ABOUT THE AUTHOR

Carrie Clickard is an internationally published author of books for children and adults. Her work ranges from science and technology to history, biography, and literature, and can be found in bookstores and journals across five countries and three languages.